# Super Goofy Jokes

*by*

**Jacqueline Horsfall**

*Illustrated by*

**Rob Collinet**

**STERLING**

New York / London

www.sterlingpublishing.com/kids

*For Dylan*

Library of Congress Cataloging-in-Publication Data

Horsfall, Jacqueline.
  Super goofy jokes / Jacqueline Horsfall ; illustrated by Rob Collinet.

      p. cm.
   Includes index.
   ISBN 1-4027-0927-7
   1. Wit and humor, Juvenile. [1. Jokes.] I. Collinet, Rob, ill. II.
Title.
PN6166 .H69 2004
818'.602--dc22

                                    2003024417

Lot #:
10  9  8  7  6  5  4  3
08/11
Published by Sterling Publishing Co., Inc.
387 Park Avenue South, New York, NY 10016

Distributed in Canada by Sterling Publishing
c/o Canadian Manda Group, 165 Dufferin Street
Toronto, Ontario, Canada M6K 3H6
Distributed in Australia by Capricorn Link (Australia) Pty. Ltd.
P.O. Box 704, Windsor, NSW 2756, Australia

Sterling ISBN 978-1-4027-7856-8

For information about custom editions, special sales, premium and
corporate purchases, please contact Sterling Special Sales
Department at 800-805-5489 or specialsales@sterlingpublishing.com.

# CONTENTS

# 1. Nature Noodles

Where do worms get their mail?
*At the compost office.*

What would you get if worms ruled the earth?
*Global worming.*

Why do lightning bugs get A's in school?
*They're very bright.*

What do frogs think of flies?
*They're toadally awesome.*

*How do lobsters get to the airport?*
*By taxi crab.*

Where do little elm trees go after kindergarten?
*Elm-mentary school.*

What kind of nuts don't grow on trees?
*Donuts.*

What does an ash tree take for a headache?
*Ash-pirin.*

What do ferns do when winter comes?
*Turn up the fern-ace.*

Why do pine trees love winter?
*They can wear their fir coats.*

What kind of tree likes doing housework?
*A sweeping willow.*

Why did the butterfly cry?
*It saw the moth bawl.*

What do you call a bee born in May?
*A Maybe.*

What insect can tell time?
*A clockroach.*

Which insects have the best manners?
*Ladybugs.*

Why shouldn't you tell secrets in a room full of beetles?
*Because the room is bugged.*

What do you call two beetle babies fighting over milk?
*A beetle bottle battle.*

How do gnats feed their young?
*Gnaturally.*

What's a flea's favorite plant?
*A cattail.*

What's a flea's second favorite plant?
*Dogwood.*

Why don't ants smell?
*They wear deodor-ant.*

What goes buzz, buzz, buzz, plop?
*A bee laughing its head off.*

What do honeybees use to check out flowers?
*Bee-noculars.*

## Wacky Nature Books

*How to Catch Butterflies* by Annette N. Ajar

*Collecting Clams and Mussels* by Shelley Beech

*How to Fetch a Pail of Water* by Jack N. Jill

*My Life as a Lumberjack* by Tim Burr

*Safe Winter Driving* by I. C. Rhodes

*Cross Country by Auto* by Phil R. Upp

*Crossing Streams* by Carey Meover

*Why Bees Love Flowers* by Polly Nation

*Strong Breezes* by Gustav Wind

*Making a Living in the Woods* by Rob N. Hood

Why did the bee go south for the winter?
*To visit an ant in Florida.*

What do butterflies become after they graduate from college?
*Mothematicians.*

How do police get rid of mosquitoes?
*They call out the SWAT team.*

What do ants furnish their homes with?
*Ant-iques.*

Which bank does the sun go to?
*Daylight Savings.*

What did summer say to spring?
*"Help! I'm going to fall!"*

How can a hurricane see where it's going?
*It has an eye in its middle.*

What do riverbanks do their homework in?
*Their notebrooks.*

What flower do you get when you cross a violin with a clarinet?
*A violet.*

Which flowers are happy to see you?
*Glad-iolas.*

If a buttercup is yellow, what color is a hiccup?
*Burple.*

Why did the hiker climb a mountain?
*To get a peak at it.*

Why don't mountains get cold in winter?
*Because they wear snowcaps.*

Why did Cinderella wish she had been magically turned into a tree?
*She wanted to be very poplar.*

Why did Mozart write his symphonies on a fallen tree?
*He was de-composing.*

Why did the silly boy take his piggy bank outdoors?
*He heard there was going to be a change in the weather.*

What should you do if you fall off your bicycle?
*Get back on and re-cycle.*

What falls on a mountain but never gets hurt?
*Snow.*

What did the mountain scream after the earthquake?
*"It wasn't my fault!"*

# 2. Animal Crackers

What kind of plane does an elephant fly?
*A jumbo jet.*

Why do grizzly bears live in caves?
*Because they can't afford apartments.*

How do reindeer kill insects?
*With their ant-lers.*

What do you call sheep that join law enforcement?
*The Fleece Police.*

What's a kangaroo's favorite year?
  *Leap year.*

Why do mother kangaroos hate rainy days?
  *Because their kids want to play inside.*

What do you call a crocodile that lives between two buildings?
  *An alley-gator.*

Why didn't the alligator finish its homework?
  *It was swamped.*

## Are We There Yet?

What kind of cars do ponies drive?
  *Mustangs.*

What kind of cars do hummingbirds drive?
  *Hum-vees.*

What kind of cars do stinging insects drive?
  *Bee M. Ws.*

What kind of cars do baby birds drive?
  *Hatchbacks.*

What kind of cars do couch potatoes drive?
  *Convertibles.*

What kind of cars do eels drive?
  *Electric ones.*

What kind of cars do bakers drive?
  *Rolls.*

What's a crocodile's favorite drink?
*Gatorade.*

Where do rabbits get their food?
*At hopping centers.*

Where do karate students get their food?
*At chopping centers.*

What kind of crackers are bad for parrots?
*Firecrackers.*

What do you call a lizard that wins the lottery?
*A chamelionaire.*

What animal is smarter than a talking parrot?
*A spelling bee.*

What kind of jokes do crows like?
*Corny ones.*

What do you call a tiger in the snow?
*A cool cat.*

What do you have to do before riding a horse named Everest?
*Mount Everest.*

What's a giraffe's favorite fruit?
*Neck-tarines.*

What do skunks become after they take a bath?
*Ex-stinked.*

What do seals wear with their bathrobes?
*Bedroom flippers.*

What kind of cat rides in an ambulance?
*A first-aid kitten.*

What happened when the cat ate a ball of yarn?
*She had mittens.*

What's a cat's favorite TV show?
*The Evening Mews.*

What do cats say when they want to go outdoors?
*"Me-out."*

When is it bad luck to have a black cat following you?
*When you're a mouse.*

How do mice revive each other?
*With mouse-to-mouse resuscitation.*

What do mice use for bad breath?
*Mousewash.*

How do chickens get into college?
*By passing their eggs-aminations.*

How can you tell if there's an elephant in your sandwich?
*You need a crane to pick it up.*

What would you get if a 50-ton duck stomped on the ground?
*An earthquack.*

What kind of dogs do vampires own?
  *Bloodhounds.*

Where do dogs and cats buy their furniture?
  *At flea markets.*

What happened when the pelican flew over the whale?
  *It had a blast.*

## Wacky Animal Books

*Why Cats Scratch* by Manny Fleeze

*Keep Your Pet Healthy* by Ray B. Shott

*How To Build a Better Mousetrap* by Kit E. Katt

*Why We Love Garbage Cans* by Al E. and Tom Katt

*Who Stole My Cheese?* by Mick E. Mowce

*Raising Bears at Home* by Claude Updewall

*Dogs Running Wild* by Ty M. Upp

What do kangaroos ask for at motels?
*Kangarooms.*

What's a cow's favorite movie?
  *"The Sound of Moooosic."*

What's a crayfish's favorite movie?
  *"Fiddler Crab on the Roof."*

What do whales use to hold their tails up?
  *Blubber bands.*

Why couldn't the baby whale use its blowhole?
  *It was only a little squirt.*

Why did the whale cross the ocean?
  *To get to the other tide.*

What's a ladybug's favorite singing group?
*The Beetles.*

Why don't crickets have antennae?
*Because they get cable.*

Where do spiders get their music?
*Off the Web.*

What kind of creatures rent videos?
*Tapeworms.*

What do you call a bird that flies into a telephone pole?
*A black-and-bluejay.*

What do you call a pig flying a helicopter?
*A pork chopper.*

What kind of spaceship do sheep fly?
*Ewe F. Os.*

# 3. People Pranksters

Why are pizza makers so wealthy?
   *They're always rolling in dough.*

Why would Snow White make a good judge?
   *She's the fairest of them all.*

What kind of car does Mickey Mouse drive?
   *A Minnie van.*

What should you do if a teacher rolls her eyes at you?
   *Pick them up and roll them back to her.*

Why did the lawyer take her iron to court?
*She had pressing business.*

What do you call a bunch of artists in a box?
*A chest of drawers.*

How did the lumberjack chop down a tree?
*Axedentally.*

What do sleepy gardeners use?
*Yawn mowers.*

## C'mon In!

How do you welcome a skydiver?
*"Glad you could drop in!"*

How do you welcome a sailor?
*"Nice to sea you."*

How do you welcome Santa Claus?
*"Make yourself at ho-ho-home."*

How do you welcome a centipede?
*"Put your feet, feet, feet, feet, feet, feet up."*

How do you welcome an angel?
*"Halo there, c'mon down!"*

How do you welcome a grizzly bear?
*"You're looking grrrrreat!"*

What did the lamp say when the owner turned it off?
*"Thanks a watt!"*

Why did everyone laugh at the biologist?
*He bent over and split his genes.*

What do scientists do after they discover a new gene?
*Cell-ebrate!*

Why did the farmer plow his field with a steam-roller?
*He wanted to grow mashed potatoes.*

## Wacky Library Books

*I Can Do Anything*  by Will Power

*How to Get Along With Your Sister*
    by Sharon Sharealike

*Jewelry Collecting*  by Pearl Nicholas

*Shakespeare's Phrases*  by Toby R. Nottaby

*The Unfinished Story*  by Cliff Hanger

*You Don't Say*  by Ida Claire

*Why Amy Walked to School*  by Mr. Bus

*Oops, I Did It Again!*  by Miss Take

*Hopelessly Lost*  by Wes D. Eggzit

*Embarrassed in the Shower*  by Kurt N. Fell

What does Farmer Darth Vader cultivate?
*His Force field.*

How did the farmer mend his jeans?
*With a cabbage patch.*

What do you call a chicken farmer?
*An eggspert.*

Where do hogs live at the North Pole?
*In pigloos.*

Why didn't your friend get the umbrella joke?
*It went right over her head.*

What did the motorcyclists ask for at the motel?
*A vroom-vrooom for two.*

What do you call a princess with a tidy house?
*Sweeping Beauty.*

What did the driver say when she couldn't stop?
*"Give me a brake!"*

Why did the helicopter pilot quit the late shift?
*It was a fly-by-night job.*

Who invented a plane that couldn't fly?
*The Wrong Brothers.*

Why don't scuba divers make good grades?
*They're always below C-level.*

What was the diver doing in his garage?
*Changing his shark plugs.*

Why did the biologist stop feeding dolphins?
*She didn't see the porpoise in it.*

Why did the two comic book characters fall in love?
*They were drawn together.*

What do you get when a police officer surprises a skunk?

*Law and odor.*

How did the police officer know the suspects stole the ketchup?

*He caught them red-handed.*

What did the conductor say to the drummer?

*"Beat it!"*

How do carpenters greet each other?

*"House it going?"*

What did the contractor say when his electrician came to work at noon?
  *"Wire you insulate?"*

Why are electricians so smart?
  *They keep up with current events.*

What do you call a genius pig?
  *Einswine.*

Why was Einstein's head wet?
  *He had a brainstorm.*

What kind of scientist invented soda pop?
  *A fizzicist.*

# 4. Silly Salad

What does an astronaut eat her spaghetti from?
*A satellite dish.*

Why did the biscuit hurry to school?
*It didn't want to miss roll call.*

Have you heard the peanut butter joke? I can't tell you—you might spread it around.

What do you get when you spill soda in a cornfield?
  *Popcorn.*

How do you know when there's a turkey in your refrigerator?
  *All the food is gobbled up.*

What animals like Mexican food?
  *Chili-con-carnivores.*

What do penguins put in their salad?
*Iceberg lettuce.*

What do ship captains put on their salad?
*Crew-tons.*

What would you get if you dropped a French fry on the sofa?
*A couch potato.*

Where did the first bakery open?
*On the yeast coast.*

What should you do with rude pepperoni?
*Give it a pizza your mind.*

Who went to the Pizza Ball?
*Cinderella Mozzarella.*

How does Humpty Dumpty sunbathe?
*Sunny-side up.*

What do you call a funny book about eggs?
*A yolk book.*

What did Humpty Dumpty say to the comedian?
*"You crack me up."*

What channel are the dancing chocolate candies on?
*M & MTV.*

What's a spider's favorite picnic food?
  *Corn-on-the-cobweb.*

How can you tell if a clock is hungry?
  *It goes back four seconds.*

What kind of cake is served in a haunted house?
  *Eye scream cake.*

What should you say to an unhappy cake?
  *"What's eating you?"*

What kind of fruit do shellfish eat?
*Crab apples.*

What's a scarecrow's favorite fruit?
*Strawberries.*

What do quarterbacks like to do at dinner?
*Pass the salt.*

What kind of salt do gymnasts use?
*Somersault.*

What do you call fifteen-year-old salt?
*A salt-teen.*

What do you get when a waiter trips?
*Flying saucers.*

Where do vegetables volunteer?
*The Peas Corp.*

Where do bad vegetables go?
*To the re-farm-atory.*

What does a porcupine put on its submarine sandwich?
*Dill prickles.*

Why are potatoes good detectives?
*They always keep their eyes peeled.*

What happened when the grape was promoted?
*It got a raisin pay.*

What's the best thing to take to the desert?
*A thirst-aid kit.*

What do alligators cook in?
*Croc-pots.*

Why do frogs have such an easy life?
*Because they eat whatever bugs them.*

## Shut the Door . . . I'm Dressing!

What dressing does Popeye put on his salad?
*Olive Oyl.*

What dressing do cowboys put on their salad?
*Ranch.*

What dressing do sad people put on their salad?
*Blue Cheese.*

What dressing do cruise directors put on their salad?
*Thousand Island.*

What dressing does a Cyclops put on its salad?
*Screamy Eyetalian.*

What dressing do nice cows put on their salad?
*Honey Moostard.*

Who wears a red cape and leaps from restaurant roofs in a single bound?
*Supperman.*

Who has friends for lunch?
*A cannibal.*

What do horseflies do when you invite them to dinner?
*They just drop in for a bite.*

How do you save an elephant drowning in hot chocolate?
*Throw in a marshmallow.*

What did the teddy bear say when offered dessert?
*"No, thanks, I'm stuffed."*

What's a chimp's favorite ice cream?
*Chunky Monkey.*

What is a second scoop of ice cream called?
*An ice cream clone.*

How do giant sequoias like their ice cream served?
*In pinecones.*

What kind of fruit leaves holes in your tongue?
*A porcupineapple.*

## Wacky Cookbooks

*The Best Pizza Ever* by Chris P. Krust

*All About Peppers* by Holly Peenyo

*Microwave Leftovers* by Luke Warmm

*Outdoor Cooking* by Barbie Q.

*Snacks for a Crowd* by Saul Ted P. Knotts

*Cooking With Butter* by Marge R. Inn

*No More Coffee!* by T. Baggs

*Yummy Christmas Treats* by Candy Kane

*My Favorite Dessert* by Dee Lishus

*Healthy Vegetables* by Artie Choke

Where do baby eagles eat?
*In high chairs.*

Why did the silly student eat his homework?
*The teacher said it would be a piece of cake.*

What would you get if potatoes took a bath?
*Soapspuds.*

What did one plate say to the other plate?
*"Lunch is on me!"*

# 5. Boo! Bloopers

Why do skeletons play piano?
*Because they don't have organs.*

Where do skeletons live?
*On dead end streets.*

Do mummies like being mummies?
*Of corpse!*

What do ghosts wash their hair with?
*Shamboo.*

What lies at the bottom of the ocean and twitches?
*A nervous wreck.*

How does a witch play loud music?
*On her broom box.*

What's a witch's favorite movie?
*Star Warts.*

What happens when a witch breaks the sound barrier?
*You hear a sonic broom.*

How do you welcome a ghost into your house?
*"Come right in and have a sheet."*

What kind of construction vehicle does a ghost drive?
*A screamroller.*

How do ghosts avoid computer eyestrain?
*They wear their spooktacles.*

What do baby ghosts turn on before they go to bed?
*Their frightlights.*

What do baby ghosts get when they fall down?
*Boo-boos.*

Why couldn't the elf play outside with the other elves?
*He had too much gnomework.*

Why was 6 afraid of 7?
*Because 7-8-9!*

Who brings Christmas presents to werewolves?
*Santa Claws.*

Why did the werewolf read *The Lord of the Rings* 50 times?
*It was hobbit-forming.*

What do Egyptian mummies eat for lunch when they go to the beach?
*Sand witches.*

How do mummies hide?
*They wear masking tape.*

What kind of boats do vampires like?
*Blood vessels.*

How do little vampires get to sleep?
*They count Draculas.*

How does Dracula tell time?
*He checks his clockroach.*

Why can't Dracula play baseball?
*He lost his bat.*

Why doesn't Dracula like garlic?
*It gives him bat breath.*

What did the bat say to its girlfriend?
*"You're fun to hang around with."*

Who did Frankenstein take to the prom?
*His ghoulfriend.*

What do you call a haunted wasp?
*A zom-bee.*

## Wacky Horror Books

*Trade-In Body Parts* by Frank N. Stein

*Halloween Pumpkin Carving* by Jack O. Lantern

*How I Scared Goldilocks* by Ted E. Bayer

*Where Is Little Red Riding Hood?*
    by I. M. DeWolf

*UFOs Are Real! By* A. Lee N. Bean

*How to Dig a Grave* by Barry D. Boddy

*Night of the Werewolf* by Harry Bakk

*Tarantulas on the Loose* by Isadore Open

*I Died of Fright* by Terry Fide

What happens when you take a picture of the Invisible Man?
*Nothing develops.*

What do you call a cloned kitten?
*A mew-tant life form.*

What does Tinkerbell ride at the amusement park?
*The fairy-go-round.*

How do you catch a fairy?
*By its fairy tail.*

How are spiders like ducks?
*They both have webbed feet.*

What would you get if two spiders wrestled?
*Scrambled legs.*

How big are centipedes?
*One hundred feet long.*

Where do you pay to use the Ogre Highway?
*At the trollbooth.*

# 6. Rap It Up, Please

Where do strawberries play their saxophones?
*At jam sessions.*

What kind of music gets playd at school?
*Class-ical.*

Who plays country music at the beach?
*The fiddler crabs.*

Where does a daffodil hear its favorite music?
*On a bloom box.*

What did the Pied Piper say when he lost his flute?
*"Oh, rats!"*

Why couldn't Little Boy Blue blow his horn?
*The sheep took it to band practice.*

What part does a grizzly sing in the church choir?
*Bearitone.*

What do you call three oaks who sing together?
*A tree-o.*

Which orchestra leader has webbed feet?
*The conducktor.*

### Band Aid

What instruments do doctors play in a band?
*Surgical ones.*

What do surgeons play in a band?
*Organs.*

What do turkeys play in a band?
*Drumsticks.*

What do shoemakers play in a band?
*Soxophones.*

What do skeletons play in a band?
*Trom-bones.*

What do you call a dad who sings and dances?
*A Pop-star.*

How is a movie like a broken leg?
*They both need a cast.*

Why couldn't the piano go home after the concert?
*It lost its keys.*

What did the mother piano say to the baby grand?
*"I don't like your tone, young man."*

What do you get when you cross a BMW with a piano?
*Car tunes.*

What do pianists use to eat their steak?
*Tuning forks.*

Why was the pianist smacking her head on the keys?
*She was playing by ear.*

Why do baseball players make good pianists?
*They have perfect pitch.*

# 7. Mall Madness

When skunks go for groceries, where do they find the best bargains?
*At shopping scenters.*

Why don't bumblebees go shopping?
*They're too buzz-y.*

What happened to the origami shop that used to be on this block?
*It folded.*

Where do ghosts shop?
*At boo-tiques.*

Where do streams buy their novels?
*At the brookstore.*

How do grizzlies try on shoes?
*Bearfoot.*

What shoes should you buy when your basement is flooded?
*Pumps.*

What did the shoe say to the foot?
*"You're putting me on!"*

What kind of sneakers do birds buy?
*Ones with vel-crow.*

Where do sailors return damaged masts?
*To the sails clerk.*

How do hummingbirds stay dry?
*They buy humbrellas.*

What do you call a kangaroo clerk with bad manners?
*Kangarude.*

How do kangaroos add up their purchases?
*With pocket calculators.*

What kind of pens do skunks buy?
*Ones with indelible stink.*

Where would you buy 36 inches?
*At a yard sale.*

What does a house buy at the mall?
*Address.*

Where should you pay your car repair bill?
*At the crash register.*

What's an easy way to double your money?
*Look at it in a mirror.*

What do pigs buy for relaxing in the backyard?
*Ham-mocks.*

# Wacky Shopping Books

*Collecting Modern Paintings* by Art X. Ibit

*Fur, Fumes, and Flowers* by Al R. Gee

*Shopping on the Second Floor* by Ellie Vader

*Out of Breath at the Food Court* by Noe S. Calator

*Department Store Courtesy* by May I. Helpyoo

*The History of Footwear* by Buck L. Myshoo

*Shoplifting: A Serious Problem*
    by Reed M. S. Wrights

Where do animals go when they lose their tails?
   *To the retail store.*

What did the duck say when she bought lipstick?
   *"Please, just put it on my bill."*

Why do department stores like cats?
*They're pre-furred customers.*

Did you hear about the two racing silkworms?
*They ended up in a tie.*

Why was the pajama store closed?
*It's only open at nightie.*

Which customers avoid early-bird sales?
*Worms.*

What's the best time to shop for sporting goods?
*Ten-nish.*

Why aren't gorillas allowed in furniture stores?
*They're always beating on their chests.*

What happens to vacuum cleaners at a busy mall?
*They get pushed around.*

## Shop Till You Drop!

What do frogs buy at the mall?
  *Open-toad sandals.*

What do clones buy at the mall?
  *Denim genes.*

What do sheep buy at the mall?
  *Baaaath towels.*

What do cats buy at the mall?
  *Purrfume.*

What do bumblebees buy at the mall?
  *Bee-kinis.*

What do chimney sweeps buy at the mall?
  *Sootcases.*

What do mummies buy at the mall?
  *Wrapping paper.*

How do billboards talk?
  *In sign language.*

How do leopards do their shopping?
  *From cat-alogs.*

Why did the bald man refuse to buy a wig?
  *He didn't want toupee.*

Why did the rabbit buy a house?
  *It was tired of the hole thing.*

Why did the rabbit get a job at the grocery store?
  *It wanted a raise in celery.*

# 8. Games & Groans

What's a baby's favorite ride?
  *A stroller coaster.*

Why was Cinderella so bad at basketball?
  *Her coach was a pumpkin.*

How does Mother Earth fish?
  *With north and south poles.*

What do petunias wear when they exercise?
  *Sweatplants.*

Why did the pecan work out?
*It was a health nut.*

How do locomotives work out?
*With personal train-ers.*

Where do trains work out?
*At the track.*

How do witches work out?
*On hexercise machines.*

How do bees start their exercises?
*With swarm-ups.*

## Hit the Deck

What card game do construction workers play?
*Bridge.*

What card game do anglers play?
*Go Fish.*

What card game do nutty ice skaters play?
*Crazy Eights.*

What card game do cardiologists play?
*Hearts.*

What card game do prisoners play?
*Solitaire.*

What's a tornado's favorite game?
*Twister.*

What game do mice like to play?
*Hide and squeak.*

What's a baby sparrow's favorite game?
*Beak-a-boo.*

If Michael Jordan gets athlete's foot, what does Santa get?
*Mistle toe.*

What do you call wood that has nothing to play with?
*Board.*

Why would you bring a trampoline to a nightclub?
*For the bouncers.*

How do surfers greet each other?
*With a tidal wave.*

# Get Going!

What do you say to a slow walnut?
*"Get cracking!"*

What do you say to a slow taxidermist?
*"Do your stuff!"*

What do you say to a slow pencil sharpener?
*"Get to the point!"*

What do you say to a slow pencil?
*"Get the lead out!"*

What do you say to a slow centipede?
*"Shake a leg, leg, leg, leg, leg!"*

What do you say to a slow rubber band?
*"Make it snappy!"*

What do waiters ask when playing tennis?
*"May I serve?"*

Why did the police go to the baseball stadium?
*They heard someone was stealing bases.*

What position do camels play on baseball teams?
*Humpire.*

Where should you sit at a ballpark if you want your clothes to get really white?
*In the bleachers.*

Why don't grasshoppers go to lacrosse games?
*They prefer cricket matches.*

Who won the race between two balls of string?
*They were tied.*

What game do falcons play on ice?
*Hawk-ey.*

Why can't a *Tyrannosaurus rex* play hockey?
*It keeps eating the goalie.*

How do frogs protect their knees when skateboarding?
*They wear lily pads.*

How do pandas ride bikes safely?
*They hold onto the handlebears.*

How do rubber bands warm up?
*They stretch.*

What exercise does your nose do when you have a cold?

*It runs.*

What exercise do you do at church?

*Knee bends.*

Where do angels swing and slide?

*At the prayground.*

What did one dumbbell say to the other?

*"Hey, weight for me!"*

# 9. Open Wide!

How did the dentist fix the dragon's teeth?
  *With a fire drill.*

What does a donkey wear to straighten its teeth?
  *Bray-ces.*

Why did the oak tree see a dentist?
  *To get a root canal.*

What does a dentist tell in court?
*"The tooth, the whole tooth, and nothing but the tooth."*

How did the snake like the doctor's joke?
*It went into hiss-terics.*

What did Mrs. Snake have at the hospital?
*A bouncing baby boa.*

Why do doctors measure snakes in inches?
*Because snakes don't have feet.*

How do you examine a sick tiger?
  *Give it a CAT scan.*

What plant do you find in emergency rooms?
  *IV.*

How do injured rubber bands get to the hospital?
  *On stretchers.*

When do houses see a doctor?
  *When they have window panes.*

Why did the basketball player go to the doctor?
  *He wanted to get more shots.*

What do birds need when they're sick?
  *Tweetment.*

When don't you feel so hot?
  *When you catch a cold.*

How can you tell if a mummy has a cold?
  *He starts coffin.*

How can you avoid getting a sharp pain in your eye
when you drink chocolate milk?
  *Take the spoon out of the glass.*

Where do dirty socks go when they get sick?
  *To the Detergency Room.*

# Wacky Medical Books

*How to Heal a Sore Throat* by Lauren Jitis

*Medical Malpractice Suits* by Sue M. Good

*Shots Don't Hurt!* by Ben Dover

*How to Write a Prescription* by Adeline Moore

*Malaria Symptoms* by Amos Quito

*Veggies for Your Health* by Brock O'Lee

*Clone Yourself!* by Gene Splitter

*Everyday Dental Care* by Pearl E. Teeth

*How to Cure Stomach Pain* by Tom E. Ake

What direction does a sneeze travel?
*Atchoo!*

Where do cows buy their cough drops?
*At the farm-acy.*

Why did the cow go to the psychiatrist?
*Because she was so moooody.*

Why can't a pony sing?
*It's always a little horse.*

Why did the fireplace call the doctor?
*The chimney had the flue.*

What sickness do rodeo riders get?
*Bronc-itis.*

Why did the germ cross the microscope?
*To get to the other slide.*

Why is an eye doctor like a teacher?
*They both test the pupils.*

What happens when an icicle falls on your head?
*It knocks you cold.*

What is a drill sergeant?
*An army dentist.*

What's the healthiest type of water?
*Well water.*

What's the perfect cure for dandruff?
*Baldness.*

What means of transportation gives people colds?
*Achoo-choo train.*

If an apple a day keeps the doctor away, what will an onion do?
*Keep everyone away.*

Why did the cookie go to the doctor?
*It felt crumby.*

Why should you tiptoe past the medicine cabinet?
*So you won't wake the sleeping pills.*

SHHHHH

How did the clock feel when no one wound it up?
*Run down.*

What would you call a small wound?
*A shortcut.*

When do you have acute pain?
*When you own a very pretty window.*

If you don't feel well, what do you probably have?
*Gloves on your hands.*

What did Captain Hook do when he lost his hand?
*He went to the second-hand shop.*

If you dropped a tomato on your toe, would it hurt much?
*Sure, if it were in a can.*

What did Frankenstein say when a bolt of lightning hit him?
*"Thanks, I needed that!"*

# 10. Computer Chuckles

What should you do if you're stuck on the Web?
*Call a spider.*

What do you call flowers that use the Internet?
*Smartyplants.*

How do we know that spiders own computers?
*They have their own websites.*

What happens when the Wicked Queen turns on her computer?
*The screen goes Snow White.*

What did one keyboard say to the other keyboard?
  *"You're not my type."*

What should you do if your computer hums?
  *Teach it the words.*

What would you get if you kept typing antidisestablishmentarianism.com into your computer?
  *Sore fingers.*

What kind of chips are found in farmers' computers?
  *Potato chips.*

How do train conductors find information on the Internet?
  *They use a search engine.*

## Weirdo Websites

Have you seen the leopard website?
*No, I haven't spotted it yet.*

Have you seen the hurricane website?
*It really blew my mind!*

Have you seen the goldfish website?
*It really bowled me over!*

Have you seen the fishing website?
*It isn't online yet.*

Have you seen the boxing website?
*It knocked me out!*

Have you seen the tomato website?
*I'll ketchup with it later.*

Have you seen the opticians' website?
*It's a site for sore eyes.*

## Weirdo Websites

Have you seen the mountain website?
*I must take a peak.*

Have you seen the paper towel website?
*It's very absorbing.*

Have you seen the boomerang website?
*You'll go back to it again and again.*

Have you seen the garbage can website?
*It's a load of rubbish.*

Have you seen the adhesive tape website?
*I can hardly tear myself away.*

Have you seen the lions and tigers website?
*I'm not wild about it.*

Have you seen the alarm clock website?
*It's very striking.*

Why do beavers spend so much time on the Internet?
*They never want to log off.*

Where do snowmen put their websites?
*On the Winternet.*

Why did the computer sneeze?
*It had a virus.*

What should you do if you find a twig in your
disk drive?
*Speak to the branch manager.*

What do you call a grandmother who designs
programs?
*A computer programma.*

## Wacky Computer Books

*How to Clean Your Computer*
  by Dusty Keebord

*Let's All Ban Spam!* by O. Kaye Bymee

*How to Fix Spelling Mistakes* by Dee Leete

*The Greatest Online Story Ever Written!*
  by Paige Turner

*Set Up Your Own Website* by Dot Comm

*How to Get a High-Tech Job* by Bea A. Nerd

*The World's Largest Software Company*
  by Mike Rosoft

How do teachers take attendance by
computer?
  *They use scroll call.*

What's a carpenter's favorite computer icon?
*The toolbar.*

What do computer programmers do on weekends?
*Go for disk drives.*

What would you get if you crossed a computer with a ballerina?
*The Netcracker Suite.*

How can you learn ballet dancing on the Internet?
*Use the tutu-torial.*

Where does an elephant keep its laptop?
*In its trunk.*

What do you get if a tarantula sits on your computer?
*A spider byte.*

How does Old MacDonald send messages?
*By e-i-e-i-o-mail.*

Why don't you stamp e-mails?
*Because your foot would go right through the screen.*

How do Italian cooks swap recipes?
*By spaghett-e-mail.*

Why was the chicken banned from sending e-mails?
*She was always using fowl language.*

How do e-books communicate?
*They page each other.*

# 11. Crazy Celebrations

What did the rabbit buy his fiancée?
*A 14-carrot ring.*

How do you keep a baby fly from crying?
*Give it a paciflyer.*

What room should you take babies to when they cry?
*To the bawl room.*

Why did Benny Bee get married?
*He finally found his honey.*

What do farmers give their wives when they marry?
*Hogs and kisses.*

What do maples give each other when they marry?
*Tree rings.*

What do hamburgers give each other when they marry?
*Onion rings.*

What did the pinky say to the thumb?
*"I think I'm in glove with you."*

What happens when two angels get married?
*They live harpily ever after.*

Who gets married at a witch's wedding?
*The bride and broom.*

What do you call two married spiders?
*Newly-webs.*

What does a duck wear to a wedding?
*A duxedo.*

Who do pelicans bring with them to weddings?
*Their gullfriends.*

How did the mushrooms like the reception?
*They had a lot of fun-gi.*

What does Hamlet eat on his birthday?
*Danish.*

What do squirrels eat on their birthdays?
*Donuts.*

What should you do if your birthday cake tastes
crunchy?
*Spit out the plate.*

## Cut the Cake!

What do mice eat on their birthdays?
*Cheesecake.*

What do rabbits eat on their birthdays?
*Carrot cake.*

What do demons eat on their birthdays?
*Devil's food cake.*

What do saints eat on their birthdays?
*Angel food cake.*

What do dwarfs eat on their birthdays?
*Shortcake.*

What do divers eat on their birthdays?
*Sponge cake.*

What do grouchy cows eat on their birthdays?
*Sour cream cake.*

What do carpenters eat on their birthdays?
*Pound cake.*

What do police eat on their birthdays?
*Cop cakes.*

What does an oyster do on its birthday?
*Shellabrate.*

What do you always get on your birthday?
*One year older.*

When do kangaroos celebrate their birthdays?
*In leap years.*

*What birthday game do cows play?*
*Moooosical chairs.*

Why didn't the skeleton go to the birthday party?
*It had no body to go with.*

Why can't monkeys send birthday presents?
*The stamps keep sliding off the bananas.*

What do you sing before a robin blows out its candles?

*"Happy Bird-day to You!"*

What do you sing when the letter U has a birthday?

*"Happy Birthday to U!"*

Who should you call if you have 100 candles on your cake?

*The fire department.*

Why do you put candles on top of a birthday cake?

*Because you can't light them if you put them on the bottom.*

What's the best thing to put into your Easter basket?

*Your hand.*

What does Santa eat first out of his Easter basket?

*Belly beans.*

What do tarantulas drink on Halloween?

*Apple spider.*

What do turkeys dress up as for Halloween?

*Gobblins.*

What do canaries do on Halloween?

*Trick or tweet!*

## Prom Night

How did Molly Mare wear her hair to the prom?
*In a ponytail.*

How did Brenda Baker wear her hair to the prom?
*In a bun.*

How did Sarah Sow wear her hair to the prom?
*In pigtails.*

How did Colleen Contortionist wear her hair to the prom?
*In a twist.*

How did Benny Bee wear his hair to the prom?
*In a buzz cut.*

# Wacky Celebration Books

*Some Day My Prince Will Come*
by Crystal Slippers

*How To Plan A Fun Party* by Will I. C. U.
Thayer

*My Favorite Easter Gift* by Pat A. Bunnee

*Too Excited to Sleep!* by Eliza Wake

*365 Simple Celebrations* by Anita Dayoff

*How I Became a Millionaire* by Nick L. N. Dyme

*The Secrets to a Long Life* by Vera Olde

*Belated Birthdays* by M. T. Handed

*Holidays from A to Z* by Dick Shenary and
Alfie Bett

Why did the silly guest take a bowl of salsa with him when he went swimming?
*His host said, "Please take a dip in my pool."*

What kind of parties do bricklayers attend?
*Cement mixers.*

Did you hear about the party in the basement?
*It made the Best Cellar List.*

What does a werewolf say when the party's over?
*"Fangs a lot for inviting me!"*

# Index